Pride of the Shires

The Story of the Whitbread Horses

by John Oaksey

Photographs/Snowdon

HUTCHINSON OF LONDON

A View of the East End of the Brewery Yard, by G. Garrard, 1792

Hutchinson & Co (Publishers) Ltd,3 Fitzroy Square, London W1

London Melbourne Sydney Auckland Wellington Johannesburg and agencies throughout the world

First published 1979
Text and illustrations © Whitbread & Co. Ltd

Set in Monophoto Baskerville by Tradespools Ltd, Frome
Printed in Great Britain by Balding and Mansell Ltd, Wisbech
Bound by Wm. Brendon and Son, Ltd, Tiptree, Essex

Designed by Roger Walker

ISBN 0 09 136240 7

WHEN Samuel Whitbread first set up a brewery in 1742 – at the corner of Whitecross Street and Old Street in the City of London – powerful heavy horses were already an essential tool of the brewer's trade. He and his partners immediately started using the best and strongest they could find and if you stand at the corner of those two London streets today you will be within an easy stone's throw of the Garrett Street stables from which fifteen Whitbread Shires are carrying on a tradition which has remained unbroken ever since.

Those first Whitbread horses were not, admittedly, known as Shires. The Oxford English Dictionary says that the word was first used in print in 1875 – in S. Sydney's *Book of the Horse* – and four years after that, when a society was finally established to encourage and regulate the breed, its first committee decided to call themselves 'The English Carthorse Society of Great Britain and Ireland'. Not altogether inappropriately that verbose and uninformative title was chosen on April Fools' Day in 1879 – its supporters arguing, against powerful opposition, that the term 'Shire' was 'known only to a few experts'. It took another four years of sometimes fairly heated argument to get the title changed to what it has been ever since, 'The Shire Horse Society'.

But in 1760, just ten years after Samuel Whitbread bought the King's Head Brewery on part of the present site at Chiswell Street, Robert Bakewell took over from his father as tenant of Dishley Grange in Leicestershire. I do not think that many would quarrel with Keith Chivers' choice of this date, 1760, as 'the beginning of Shire history', because Bakewell immediately began to devote much of his many-sided genius as a livestock breeder to the improvement of the Leicestershire Black Heavy Horse. Impressed by the Frisian stallions and mares already brought to England by the Earls of Chesterfield and Huntingdon, he set out for West Friezland and, after a good deal of haggling with the understandably reluctant Dutch, came home in triumph with six mares. The matings which he then arranged between these matriarchs and his own Black stallions were the foundation on which, by skilful and intensive in-breeding, he 'fixed' the type for which the name of Dishley soon became famous wherever men cared about heavy horses.

Partly perhaps because of the prevalent religious scruples about in-breeding of any kind, Bakewell, a devout Unitarian, was remarkably uncommunicative about his breeding methods. If any written records were kept they have not survived and it seems probable that, apart from Bakewell himself, Will Peet, his stud groom at Dishley for nearly forty years, may have been the only other man who knew which stallion sired which foal.

Although Bakewell seldom actually sold his stallions – preferring to let them out for a season's round – there is no doubt that his efforts had far-reaching results. In 1774, for instance, 'a remarkable strong black horse' and 'a beautiful black horse . . . allowed to be the best ever shown in Scotland' were advertised in an Edinburgh paper to cover mares at a fee of fifteen shillings. One was said to be 'bred by Mr. Bakewell at Dishley in Leicestershire' and the other was 'the property of Mr. Robert Bakewell'. So, although there is to my knowledge no actual proof, it seems a reasonable guess that in 1787, when George III visited the Chiswell Street Brewery, some of the eighty horses by whom, according to the *London Chronicle*, he and Queen Charlotte were so much impressed, may well have had Dishley blood in their veins.

Of course, in those days brewers used horses for many other tasks besides pulling drays. Not long before the Royal visit 'a stupendous steam engine' designed by James Watt had been installed at Chiswell Street for grinding malt. It had taken the place of seventy horses who were till then employed, six at a time, to turn the grinding wheel. So most of the eighty animals George III inspected were certainly dray-horses.

The size, make and shape of any horse in the distant past must always be to some extent a matter of guesswork but here we have at least two clues. One is a picture painted by George Garrard in 1792 of a Whitbread gelding being backed between the shafts of a dray in the Brewery yard. The other is a Whitbread groom's proud boast to George III – reported again by the *London Chronicle* that day in 1787. 'Yielding to the harmless vanity of his office', the *Chronicle*'s somewhat pompous reporter wrote, 'he said he would shew His Majesty "the highest horse among his subjects".' The *Chronicle* then goes on to describe the King's 'accurate guess' at the horse's height 'which was really remarkable, no less than seventeen hands and three inches'.

Well, admittedly, if the horse in Garrard's picture stood anything like seventeen-three then either the man at his head was a giant or the artist's sense of proportion was at fault. But that, with all due respect to Mr. Garrard, is quite a feasible explanation. As Keith Chivers writes, 'to study horse breeds by looking at the works of the great masters is about as sensible as trying to learn history by reading Shakespeare'. Of course he had much earlier 'masters' in mind and we must not be unfair to Mr. Garrard. Apart from the comparative size of the man and one or two other details (the drays now used do not have shafts so the horses, who nowadays work in pairs, do not usually need saddles) his picture might almost have been painted at Chiswell Street today.

Whatever he looked like, the horse described in the *London Chronicle* would, at least in terms of size, have suited Whitbreads' present horse foreman Charlie Ruocco. Seventeen-two is the minimum height he now demands when paying £1000 or thereabouts for a four- or five-year-old Shire gelding.

But before describing the lives those geldings lead and the stable which Charlie so benevolently controls I should perhaps use the Brewery's foundation in the eighteenth century as a staging post from which to look back at the early history of the heavy horse in Britain – and forward to the present day.

War, as we shall see, has affected the heavy horse in many different ways – sometimes encouraging his production and improvement, sometimes preventing it altogether and sometimes causing short-lived 'booms' followed, all too often, by a violent slump. For most of recorded history warhorses of all kinds have suffered dreadfully in the service of their misguided masters. But at least a war – or at any rate an invasion – can claim to have brought us the 'great' or heavy horse in the first place. Needless to say there were horses in England long before the Battle of Hastings and, judging by Julius Caesar's description of those who pulled the ancient Britons' chariots, they were brave, hardy and manoeuvrable. But in the eleventh century and throughout the Middle Ages those admirable qualities – of which Prince Rupert and Oliver Cromwell were to make such deadly use – had become much less important on the battlefield than the size, weight and strength to carry an armoured knight.

Mr Whitbread's Wharf, by G. Garrard

I honestly don't know how many horses King Harold had at Hastings but feel that any who were there deserve our sympathy. For one thing, some of them had travelled to York and back in just over ten weeks – fighting another battle on the way – and for another they must have felt (and certainly looked) like ponies beside the Spanish and Norman Destriers or heavy warhorses on which William the Conqueror's knights and gentlemen-at-arms were mounted. It may be an oversimplification to call Hastings a battle in which the cavalry beat the infantry, but the English, weary and outnumbered, were also heavily outhorsed and the longbow which was to restore the balance of power so dramatically at Crécy and Agincourt had not yet been developed.

Nor had the practice of gelding male horses. Destriers (the name, used for any warhorse at the time of Hastings, later came to mean those which were trained specially for jousting) were all stallions so it was inevitable that they should have an influence on the native English breed when William divided up the conquered land between their knightly owners. In any case, the Normans knew how vital heavy warhorses were to their military power and

some of them, quite probably with royal encouragement, imported Continental stallions with the specific object of breeding them on their English estates.

One of the few whose name we know was a singularly unattractive character called Robert de Bellême whose father had been one of William's most powerful and favoured followers. On his father's death in 1094 (followed with almost suspicious alacrity by that of his eldest brother Hugh) Robert succeeded to vast estates both in Normandy and England – and proceeded to govern their unfortunate inhabitants from a castle near Bridgnorth with a horrid mixture of cruelty, rapacity and greed.

By 1102 he seems finally to have gone too far – even by the rough and ready standards of those feudal days. In response to an agonised petition citing 'forty-five dire and grievous charges' Henry I brought an army to the borders and threw Robert forcibly out of England. History does not relate exactly what happened to this loathsome-sounding man but throughout his reign of terror he had been setting up breeding establishments and the only good thing ever remembered about him was his stallions.

In modern times the sort of character you associate with the Shire is a little like Robert's horse – large, calm and determined but essentially good natured, possibly stubborn but certainly slow to anger. So it is strange that the next man after Robert de Bellême whom we know to have imported heavy stallions from the Continent on a large scale is King John, perhaps the least admirable character ever to sit on the English throne. In 1200, fifteen years before he was forced much against his will to sign Magna Carta, John imported no less than a hundred stallions from the low countries and distributed them carefully in what he considered suitable centres for breeding around the country. Although the stallions possibly did not cover as many mares in those days as some of them do now the size of this influx must have had a tremendous effect. Although, again, we can only guess at their size, these Flemish stallions were almost certainly black, like their descendants, and probably more hairy-legged than the Destriers who came over with William. So it requires no outlandish stretch of the imagination to regard them as the mediaeval founders of the line which ran through Robert Bakewell's Leicestershire Blacks to the Shire of the present day.

Despite King John's efforts however, demand for heavy horses continued to exceed supply for most of the fifteenth and sixteenth centuries. Edward II lost hundreds of the precious beasts either killed or captured in the disaster of Bannockburn and for many years thereafter – years of unceasing strife along the Scottish border – it was a felony to sell or export horses of any kind to Scotland. Documents dating from the time of Bannockburn show in fact that stallions were being peacefully led around Shropshire and adjoining counties for the purpose of covering mares. Luckily for them they belonged to the many nobles who took such a poor view of Edward's favourite Piers Gaveston that they refused to travel with him for the attempted relief of Stirling – and therefore missed the carnage of Bannockburn.

The breeding of horses of all sorts – and especially of those suitable for battle – was severely discouraged by the Wars of the Roses. It is one thing to produce horses to fight for your King and country abroad, but quite another to breed them at home when the ebb and flow of a civil war may all too easily force you to make an involuntary present of your stock to the other side.

So, by the end of the Plantagenet era, the nation's stock of heavy horses had dwindled yet again. If Shakespeare is right that the last Plantagenet, Richard III, cried out 'My Kingdom for a horse' on Bosworth Field, his victorious successor Henry Tudor may soon have felt like echoing those words. Henry promptly passed a law to prohibit the export of *all* stallions but unfortunately an exception was made for owners who wished to take their own horses abroad with them and 'promised not to sell them'. So many of these appear to have been 'lost' – or 'stolen' by rapacious foreigners – that the Act was almost entirely a failure.

Henry VIII improved that situation slightly by increasing the penalties for 'export' but his other attempts at encouraging breeders and improving the breed were mostly a chaotic failure. One of his laws 'compelled' landowners with a certain acreage to keep a corresponding number of mares and another made it illegal to let out stallions under a certain height – fifteen hands in some counties and fourteen in others. Do not forget that except for the great parks the countryside was still not at all widely enclosed or split up into fields. One undersized stallion on the loose could do a great deal of damage but since each owner was allowed one 'unavoidable escape' without penalty each year this law too was pretty ineffective. Orders were also given for an annual round-up of all mares and fillies after which any of them 'thought not likely to grow or to be able to bear foals of reasonable stature' were to be killed. No definition of 'reasonable stature' was laid down and since all differences of opinion had to be resolved at quarter sessions I imagine the round-ups did more good to lawyers than anyone else.

Neither Edward VI nor Queen Mary had any great effect upon the world of horses except by passing harsher laws against those who stole them.

Although Queen Elizabeth still further increased penalties for exporting to Scotland, 'the decay of horses within the realm' was so great that when the Spanish Armada put to sea only 3000 cavalry could be mustered in defence throughout England. Luckily the glories of the first Elizabethan Age were sustained by sailors, not by horsemen. But two things happened in Elizabeth's reign which are very relevant to the story. First, the Queen herself acquired a coach. She probably regretted it because, after travelling to Warwick in 1572 behind six horses (the biggest available), she found herself 'unable to sit down for several days'. But, although there were no roads to speak of and the 'carriages' had no springs of any kind, the Queen's example was widely and promptly followed. According to one account it took 400 teams (a total of 2400 horses) to move the Queen and her court from one place to another and although pack-horses were still widely used the change from carrying to pulling had begun. The heavy horse had acquired a new role – basically the same one which the Whitbread Shires still play on the streets of London.

But horses of their size and strength were non-existent in Elizabethan England – and so was the fertile land on which in the eighteenth century and thereafter that size and strength was to be acquired. No attempt had yet been made to drain the Fenlands of East Anglia. The last thing you wanted on their soggy treacherous surface was a 'heavy horse' of any sort. In 1565 in fact an Act was passed reducing the minimum height for stallions in the Fens to *thirteen hands*. But ironically enough, only thirty-six years later

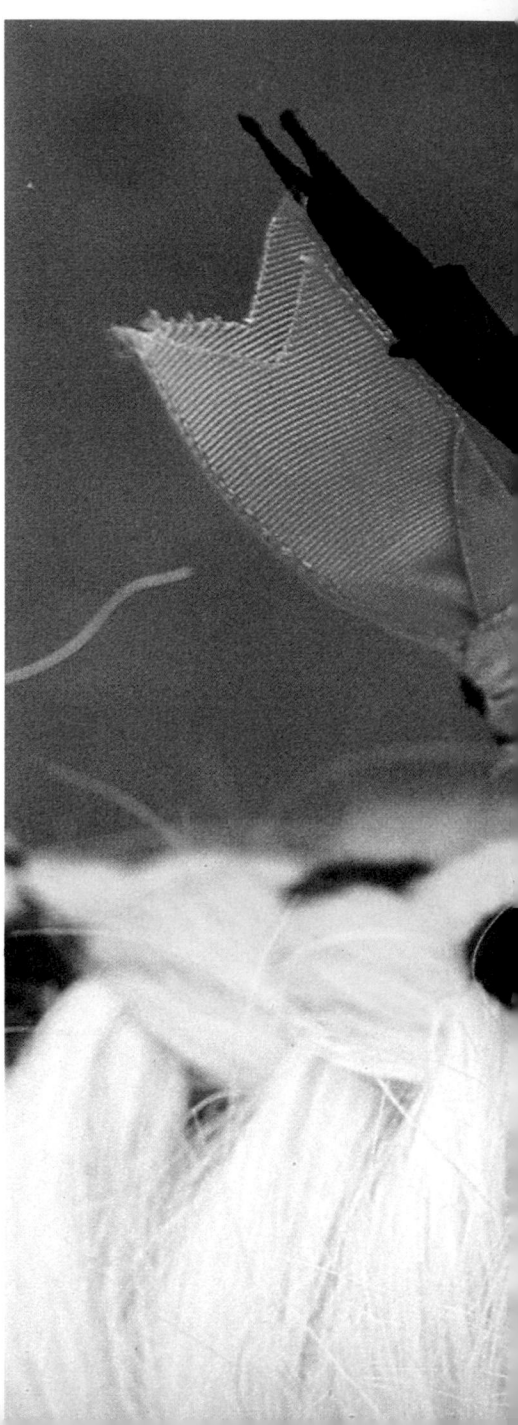

Parliament passed another Act which appointed commissions to start the drainage operations which, over the next century and a half, were to transform those same Fens into a uniquely fertile nursery for animals in general and heavy horses in particular.

That same one hundred and fifty years – between Queen Elizabeth's death and George III's accession in 1760 – saw the final departure of the 'great' or heavy horse from the battlefield. Unfortunately for him he continued, in his new draft-horse role, for nearly two more centuries to transport the materials and weapons of war – and therefore, all too often, suffered its savagery. But thanks to two very different commanders, Prince Rupert and Oliver Cromwell (who were themselves following the example of the Swedish King Gustavus Adolphus), the English Civil War so revolutionised cavalry tactics that the massive 'great horse' carrying a heavily armoured knight into battle at a ponderous trot became as much an anachronism as the invention of gunpowder had made the bow and arrow.

Gunpowder was in fact partly responsible for the change. Armour could not save you from a cannon or musket ball and,

against the inaccurate weapons of those days, the best protection of all was speed. That suited Prince Rupert and his Cavaliers, mounted as they were on horses which probably bore a much closer resemblance to modern heavyweight hunters than to Shires. Rupert taught them to charge at a gallop, relying on their impetus to break the enemy line. It worked superbly but, alas for the Royal cause, the Cavaliers had more courage and dash than discipline or common sense. Again and again their charges carried them on too far and it was left to Cromwell to mould the Ironsides into a controlled, decisive and deadly weapon. Having most of the Eastern counties under his control, Cromwell, himself a Huntingdonshire man, probably gained access, as the war continued, to bigger and stronger horses. But they had to be able to gallop and when Cromwell referred, in a letter quoted by Keith Chivers, to 'that Black you won at Horncastle' he almost certainly meant a horse which combined strength and solidity with at least adequate speed. The horse in question (which had caught the eye of Cromwell's son) may well have been a Frisian. For although the drainage of the Fens was interrupted by the Civil War, the Dutch engineers who had been engaged by King Charles I to undertake it certainly brought both Frisian and Flemish horses with them to East Anglia.

In the hundred years which followed the restoration of King Charles II (a king who took more interest in the thoroughbred than any other type) attempts were undoubtedly made to produce heavier, stronger horses – if only because weight and strength were so badly needed to drag primitive unsprung coaches or wagons along the muddy tracks which passed for roads. With few exceptions however these would-be heavy horse breeders were humble men whose names and successes have not survived. William of Orange imported some big black stallions from his native Holland and although Lord Chesterfield was far more noted for diplomacy and wit than for dedication to horseflesh, he, and later the Earl of Huntingdon, did import the Frisian mares and stallions which inspired Robert Bakewell in the second half of the eighteenth century.

That brings us back to the point at which Bakewell was established at Dishley Grange. George III was on the throne and Samuel Whitbread's beer (or, to be more accurate, porter) was being towed away from Chiswell Street by horses like the one in Garrard's painting.

Now for the first time it becomes possible to get some idea from contemporary writing of those horses and of the men who bred and used them. There were, it seems, two basic, more or less generally recognised types, each known by several different names. On one side we have the Suffolk, Sorrel or Punch and on the other the Leicestershire, Black or Dray-horse. It was of course from the latter that the Shire has developed and, although descendants can be traced back to a stallion known as The Packington Blind horse (foaled in 1755 or thereabouts), a much more historically significant moment came in 1766 when Bakewell's most famous stallion 'K' (he called almost all his horses simply by letters) was foaled at Dishley Grange.

William Marshall, who with Arthur Young was the most assiduous and prolific equine 'historian' of the time, called 'K' the handsomest Black he had ever seen. 'A man of moderate size seemed to shrink behind his fore-end, which rose so perfectly upright that his ears stood (as Mr. Bakewell says every horse's ought to stand) perpendicularly over his fore feet.'

Though reluctant even at this respectful distance to give the great man an argument I would have thought this a requirement calculated to produce horses undesirably 'straight in front'. That is probably the typically ignorant comment of someone whose small knowledge of conformation is limited to racehorses and steeplechasers. But I am glad to say that in this respect, 'ears perpendicularly over fore feet', Whitbreads' present Shires would not entirely satisfy Mr. Bakewell!

Marshall expressly preferred 'K' to a younger Dishley stallion 'G' whom Bakewell 'had the honour of showing to His Majesty and who was afterwards shown publicly in London'. We have no way of knowing whether Samuel Whitbread ever saw 'G' – or for that matter any of Bakewell's horses, but their fame was spreading so fast that no one keen about and needing the best in heavy horses could easily ignore it.

In the second half of the eighteenth century the Fens, now fully drained, superbly fertile – and receiving regular infusions of Flemish blood – had begun to develop horses of a size and weight never before seen in England.

In Derbyshire and Leicestershire the Blacks were a little smaller, not so heavy but blessed with finer heads, much better, harder bone and less hair on their legs. It was on a blend of these two types that Bakewell and his successors began to build.

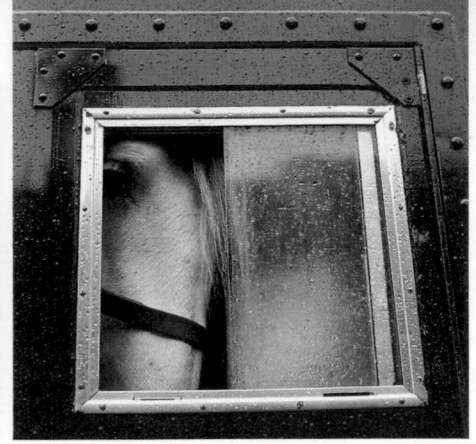

W HEN Robert Bakewell and Samuel Whitbread died – within eight months of one another in October 1795 and June 1796 – each left behind him a flourishing enterprise. But, although Whitbreads' Brewery continued to thrive and has done so ever since, the Napoleonic Wars and the years which followed them were a disastrous period for the heavy horse to whose improvement Bakewell had dedicated so much time and ingenuity.

In fact peace did more damage than war because as soon as the battered nations of Europe began to settle down behind their rearranged frontiers a huge demand sprang up across the Continent for heavy horses of all kinds. It soon became clear that England, the only European country not to have suffered invasion, had not only the most plentiful supply available but had also, thanks to Bakewell and his imitators, developed horses of a size, strength and quality not easily to be found elsewhere. So, from all over Europe, the would be purchasers came hammering eagerly on the doors of English breeders and, as bad luck would have it, this sudden boom in demand coincided with a period of deep depression in English farming. With all other sources of income shrinking or disappearing altogether the temptation to accept a good price for horses was irresistible to many impoverished farmers. So huge numbers were sold abroad – not only working geldings but mares and stallions, too, among them many of the fine Blacks whom Bakewell had worked so hard to develop. No attempt, official or unofficial, was made to stop or slow down this outpouring of precious blood. The Government either did not know or did not care and no society or other organisation had yet been formed to maintain and improve domestic breeds of horses. So the maintenance of quality was left to those stubborn, dedicated breeders who quietly refused to sell, kept themselves to themselves and continued to breed from the sort of mares and stallions Bakewell had left behind him. Sheer size and weight were uniformly preserved only in the Fens, where in fact the number of draught horses being bred rose steadily throughout the nineteenth century. However, Bakewell had rightly despised their lack of quality, and would have nothing to do with them. Their turn for improvement was not to come until the end of the century.

Samuel Whitbread II had died in the year of Waterloo but his sons carried on and one of them, W. H. Whitbread, was, like his modern namesake, both a connoisseur of horses and an active whip and horseman. In the 1830s he started the Bedford Times Stage Coach which used to cover the distance between the Blue Boar, Holborn and the Swan at Bedford at an average of ten and half m.p.h., including stops. Whitbread himself often took the reins and he would certainly have approved of his twentieth-century descendant Colonel W. H. (Bill) Whitbread who not only got round in two Grand Nationals but also inspired and founded the

first great commercially sponsored steeplechase, the Whitbread Gold Cup.

I do not of course suggest that the Bedford Times Stage Coach (which survived until overrun by the railways in 1848) was pulled by Shires – whose many qualities do not include the ability to average ten and a half m.p.h. over long distances.

But we have some first-hand evidence as to the size and quality of the heavy horses which W. H. Whitbread and his brother Samuel did maintain to do the Brewery's work at Chiswell Street. That gossipy old diarist Thomas Creevey had been a friend of their father's and was taken on a gaslit tour of the Brewery after dinner at Chiswell Street in 1823. 'A stable brilliantly illuminated containing ninety horses worth fifty or sixty guineas apiece', he wrote, 'is a sight to be seen nowhere but in this tight little island.'

I am not sure how much faith we can put in Mr. Creevey's valuations but his next comment suggests that, in size and temperament if not in price, the Whitbread horses may not have changed all that much in the last one hundred and fifty years. He praised their 'beauty and amiability' and, by the sound of it, he and his friends had put those qualities to a pretty searching test. 'Such as were lying down we favoured with sitting upon', he wrote, 'four or five of us upon a horse.'

I don't know what Gilbert, Sullivan and company would think of being sat upon by four or five well-lubricated revellers – and Charlie Ruocco would certainly never allow such frivolous interference with their beauty sleep. But it takes a large horse as well as a docile one to accommodate 'four or five men' – and this is not the only proof we have that Whitbreads were already using massive horses.

In 1802 an article in the Union magazine had described the Whitbread horses as 'of very large size' and said that the four shoes of one weighed a 'total of twenty-four pounds'. When Johnny Walker and his assistant farrier Derek Wheeler shoe a horse at the Garrett Street forge nowadays the horse shoes (a set of which lasts only about three weeks on modern tarmac roads) weigh four pounds each. So even if the metal used was heavier in the nineteenth century a six pounds shoe suggests a very considerable foot!

In that century, and for much of the twentieth, what's more, the brewery horse had to cart malt from the docks and, later, from the railway stations. As Keith Chivers discovered when talking to Robert Daplyn – who was a horse keeper with Whitbreads from 1900 until he retired aged seventy-three in 1955 – malt wagons took a great deal more pulling than even a fully loaded dray. The wagons themselves weighed two tons empty and they carried four tons of malt. Though designed for four horses they were pulled by only two and in Daplyn's time each pair delivered at least three loads a day. It was no job for weaklings.

The agricultural slump which followed the Napoleonic Wars was itself followed by a boom in which both arable and livestock farming suddenly began to show big profits. With the introduction of much improved agricultural machinery the horse had by now taken over almost completely from the ox as the chief source of power on the land. But although, as a result, more farm horses were needed than ever before, most of the breeders who supplied them were not, by a very long chalk, Robert Bakewells. Nor, with some notable exceptions, were they even trying to produce the kind of dray-horse in which any self-respecting brewer could take pride.

The horses they did produce were, as Keith Chivers writes in disgust, 'mostly mongrels'. What we would now call Shires were freely mixed with Suffolks, half-breds or even thoroughbreds. Big, heavy-topped 'showy' stallions were mated with mares too small or unsound to work in the fields themselves and although many of the results were no doubt strong enough to plough or pull a muck-cart, they were ill-suited to long hours of work in the rough, smoky streets of the new industrial England.

Plagued from the start by weakness, faulty conformation and the various kinds of unsoundness to which it led, a large majority of town horses were, moreover, treated with a mixture of ignorance and neglect which all too often amounted to downright cruelty. The countryside was so much quieter and more peaceful in those days that the shock of arrival in a noisy town must have been far harder for a young horse to bear. And if he survived that there was worse, much worse to follow – bad food, bad stabling, inefficient grooming, incompetent shoeing and in many cases gross overwork. According to a parson called John Wilson who wrote about horses in 1849, 'Britons have the atrocious reputation of being the most cruel nation in Europe'.

He may have exaggerated slightly but in fact, although the R.S.P.C.A. had been founded in 1824, it was only in the last quarter of the century that ordinary people began to care about the plight of horses in the towns. Anyone who has cried his or her eyes out over *Black Beauty* can imagine the effect of Anna Sewell's classic on a sentimental Victorian public in 1877. But, deep though its impact may have been on those who read it, the general attitude to working horses still contained precious little kindness or compassion. I am glad to be able to record, however, that even the critical Reverend Wilson seems to have agreed that, as a rule, brewers looked after their horses a great deal better than most. He admired (as I have in the stables at Garrett Street) 'the facility with which their horses will back a wagon into a narrow street or archway but a few inches wider than the vehicle itself'. Another writer, William Miles, praised the Brewers in the 1860s for their custom of having worn-out horses destroyed, instead of selling them on for a pittance to other poorer and less considerate owners.

It is not clear exactly when Whitbreads adopted their modern custom of retiring old horses to suitable homes in the country but back in 1750, only eight years after founding the Brewery, Samuel Whitbread had bought twenty-eight acres of land at Barkingside. His purpose was to have some convenient handy grass on which the Brewery's horses could be turned out for a summer rest and that tradition is still maintained when a number of Shires are sent each summer from London for a 'holiday with hay' on the Company's hop farm at Paddock Wood in Kent. Gilbert and Sullivan, Shield (who has alas since died) and Armour, Winston and Warrior and Pikeman and Musketeer all enjoyed that privilege in 1978.

Lord Snowdon's pictures show more clearly than any words how the feel of grass under their feet goes to the big horses' heads. In his *Memoirs of a Foxhunting Man*, Siegfried Sassoon described his own reaction to the sight of Paddock Wood. 'I felt that almost anything might happen in a world which could show me twenty hop-kilns neatly arranged in a field'. It is a pity he was never, so far as we know, at the farm on a morning when the Shires were turned out for their holiday, because they clearly feel too that 'anything

might happen'. Some pretend to be racehorses, others prefer the role of a bucking bronco – and all of them are transformed from sober, respectable, hard-working city gentlemen into huge irresponsible school boys. And then, after a few magnificent minutes, they settle down to munch away peacefully in the sun.

For the reasons already given it became more and more difficult throughout the first three-quarters of the nineteenth century to find and buy horses strong and sound enough to stand up to long hours of work in London. But some of the right type were still being bred and the fact that Whitbreads provided horses for the Speaker of the House of Commons' coach (originally built for Queen Anne) at various times from 1839 onwards seems to suggest that the Brewery managed to maintain its equine standards. Admittedly, the first Speaker to use Whitbread horses, C. Shaw Lefevre, later Viscount Eversleigh, was a partner in the company. But many

Speakers since have followed his example and a pair of grey Whitbread Shires has pulled the coach at all the major State occasions of this century including both the Coronation and, most recently, the Jubilee processions of our present Queen.

'I have always considered that the substitution of the Internal Combustion Engine for the horse marked a very gloomy passage in the progress of mankind.'

Many lovers of the horse in general and of the Shire in particular would wholeheartedly agree with Winston Churchill's famous dictum – but that 'gloomy passage' was still some way ahead in the middle of the nineteenth century. Agriculture was booming, the quality of cattle and sheep bred in Britain was steadily being raised and the gloomy truth had to be faced that the heavy horse was just about the only farm animal who had, if anything, deteriorated in the past hundred years.

In the 1870s however two more or less unconnected things occurred. The golden years of agricultural prosperity came to an abrupt and painful end – and a movement began at long last to regulate and encourage the scientific breeding of Shire horses. There was still argument about whether to call them 'Shires' but, although not at first adopted as the name of the breed's society, the word Shire was at least now commonly used by experts to distinguish this particular type of heavy horse from his Scottish cousin (some would say descendant) the Clydesdale and from the much more distinguishable Suffolk.

All three breeds began to organise stud books and societies for the first time within the same eleven months – partly no doubt through an understandable desire not to be beaten to the draw but also partly because of a large and ominous influx of horses from Belgium in the early 1870s. This was quite rightly regarded as an insult and a challenge and dedicated men such as Frederick Street, Edward Coke, Walter Gilbey and the Earl of Ellesmere set about forming 'the English Carthorse Society'. The story of their activities and of the Shire horse stud book's early days is told with wit as well as scholarship by Keith Chivers in *The Shire Horse*, a definitive record which I can wholeheartedly recommend to anyone interested in the subject.

Early attempts to trace and document the origins of the breed were badly hampered by an almost total absence of records, but it is fascinating to learn from Mr. Chivers that every single one of the 228 Shire colt foals born in the years 1969 to 1973 were descended in direct male line from a brown horse called Harold which won the Championship at the London Spring Show in 1887. Harold had in fact come within an ace of being sold to America but was rescued in the nick of time by Sir Henry Allsopp who later sold him to a Mr. A. C. Duncombe. Duncombe owned another stallion called Premier and the combination of blood from these two – Harold on a mare by Premier or Premier on a mare by Harold – contributed hugely to what Keith Chivers calls 'the golden age' of Shire horse history – the fourteen years immediately before the First World War.

The influence of another great foundation sire called William the Conqueror had by this time faded out altogether. So, looking back to the beginning of the story at the Battle of Hastings, Harold may be said to have had the last laugh.

But by far the greatest achievement of the Shire Horse Society (as it was called after 1883) has been the improvement it wrought in the breed – above all in terms of soundness and freedom from the many infirmities to which, for most of the nineteenth century, the heavy horse was heir. The first annual London Show at Islington in 1880 was a crucial landmark because a clause in the judges' rules enforced the automatic rejection of any stallion who, however handsome in other respects, suffered from a weakness which he might communicate to his offspring. This policy was faithfully followed at shows all over the country and in the forty years before the Great War hereditary forms of weakness like roaring, sidebones, spavins and ringbone were as a result largely eliminated. The Society also encouraged local groups to hire suitable stallions for covering mares belonging to their members and in 1918 at the Society's insistent request the Ministry of Agriculture began to licence stallions for soundness. By 1921 in fact, from more than 2500 Shire applicants for a licence only just over ten per cent were refused on grounds of unsoundness.

Howerever much the formation of a breed society may have improved his general soundness and conformation the Shire still had a battle to fight in the 1920s and 30s, for the internal combustion engine was well on the way now to achieving the mechanical transformation which Winston Churchill so rightly called 'a very gloomy passage in the progress of mankind'. In towns and fields alike lorries and tractors had begun to give the Shire and all his draught horse cousins deadly serious competition.

On balance, and considering what has happened since, the horse must be said to have kept his end up amazingly well in the period between the wars. His fortunes, like those of the whole country, sank to their lowest ebb around 1930, but by 1939 he had achieved, if not by any means a complete recovery, at least a remarkable effort at survival. This was due partly to his own qualities, partly to the faults of his mechanical opponents and partly to factors over which neither of them had control. For one thing, the early tractors had various weaknesses. They were understandably unreliable; until the invention of pneumatic tyres they could not be moved from place to place by road and almost all existing agricultural machinery had been designed for use with horses, not with tractors. In any case their initial cost was so great (though not nearly as great as it is now) that only the biggest farms could afford them. Then, as now, you could argue all night about the comparative cost of running horses and tractors – the cost, that is, of fodder on one side, of fuel on the other and of human labour on both. But throughout the period between the wars horse fodder was cheaper than petrol and oil and labour both in town and country was very cheap indeed. The fact that the horse ate the product of British farms and provided more work for British workmen seemed in those years of depression and unemployment powerful arguments in his favour.

You might have expected the horse to be more quickly and completely replaced by motor transport in the towns, and to some extent this did happen. But urban mechanisation was also desperately expensive and therefore, during the depression, desperately slow.

As early as 1925 a campaign was launched in the press to ban the use of horses on various London streets. Some such bans were imposed in the thirties but there was not, I am glad to hear, much support for a proposal, in the House of Lords of all places, that horses should be licensed and that, as each one died, the licence should not be re-issued for a replacement!

The standard of lorries does not seem to have improved as fast as that of tractors, and although obviously preferable for long journeys, they could not (and, at least arguably, still cannot) compete with the horse for the kind of short-haul town work which involves a lot of stops, long waits and manoeuvring in small spaces and openings which were designed for horses rather than machines in the first place.

With many such jobs still needing to be done in London there was never any question of Whitbreads giving up their Shires. Nonetheless, numbers were inevitably reduced – from over four hundred before the first war to fifty or sixty in 1939. But in that year, as Keith Chivers writes, 'the horse world was turned upside down'. It took the internal combustion engine *and* Adolph Hitler to strike the blow but together they very nearly succeeded in making it a fatal one.

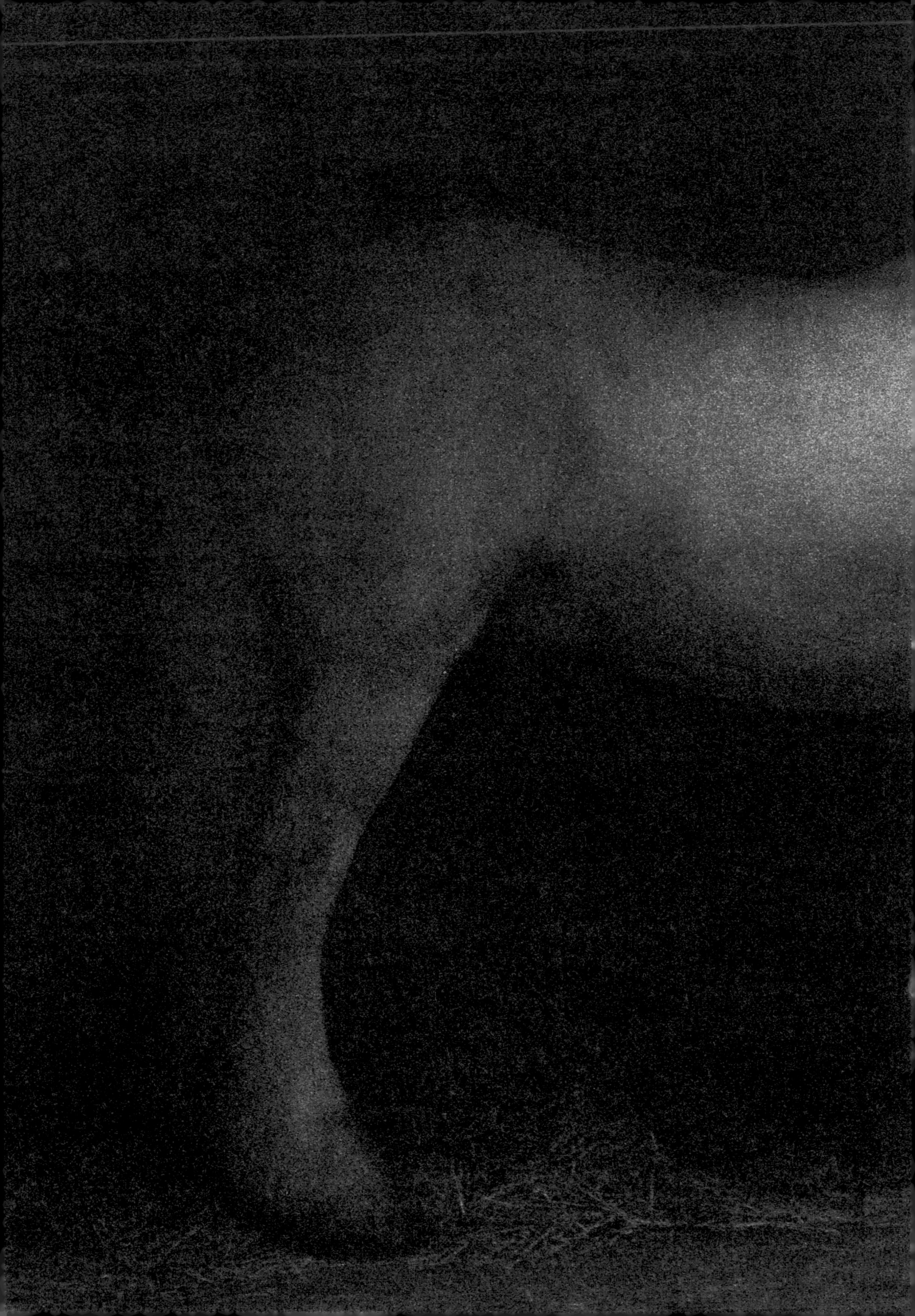

The story of one family gives a clear and gruesome picture of how things were for the heavy horse breeder in 1939. James Forshaw had started keeping stallions in 1863 and at the outbreak of war his two sons had seventy-five Shires all licensed by the Ministry – which in that same year suspended its grants to stallion owners. The Forshaw horses had been valued at a total of £15,000 but there was no food to feed them. Most of them went directly to the knacker at £3 a head. The fruit of nearly eighty years' devoted care and skill was demolished overnight.

But if the war was bad it was nothing to what came after and 1947 can surely lay dismal claim to being the blackest year in Shire horse history – indeed in the history of any British working horse. 'War ended, things settled down – then "wham",' Keith Chivers quotes an eloquent horseman's description and 'wham' is as good a word as any when a whole quiverful of slings and arrows arrive on the same target at the same time. It was all very well for the Shire Horse Society President William Cumber to say in 1947 that there were 'only twenty per cent less horses now than in 1939'. Maybe that was true when he said it, in March, but by the end of the year 100,000 horses had been put down. At least that number went the same way in 1948 and according to Chivers forty per cent of these were under three years old. With a very few honourable exceptions there was simply and suddenly no demand for them any more, either in the towns or on the land. In the towns a few brewers, Whitbreads among them, remained staunchly faithful but on the land the stalwarts became even fewer and farther between. Farm labour was getting both scarce and more expensive. Reduced minimum working hours made horses seem impractical and the farmers themselves were so much better off that for a vast majority the answer seemed to be at least one tractor. For the tiny handful of Shire breeders who obstinately continued operating the small but reliable market provided by the breweries must have seemed a rock, solid in a stormy sea.

In 1955 there were only sixty-eight Shire horses – apart from geldings in harness classes – at the Spring show and I do not think it irrelevant to note that this was the very year in which Whitbreads were first asked to provide a six-horse team of grey Shires for the Lord Mayor's coach. As Colonel Whitbread remembers it, the request came chiefly because a previous Lord Mayor had been run away with – and his successor did not feel that this was a desirable feature of the famous show! Robert Daplyn, in whose last year as foreman the invitation came, told Keith Chivers that the contractors who had hitherto horsed the coach were now having to hire both horses and men to look after them – with the result that the horses and men were a motley lot.

Talking of being run away with (which I have sometimes been on Colonel Whitbread's horses) he also remembers a rather frightening occasion before the war when the Speaker's coach was to take part in a procession *down* St. James's Street – presumably in those days not, as it is now, a one-way street uphill. Knowing that there were no brakes on the coach, Bill Whitbread arranged an early morning dress rehearsal – probably with Daplyn to assist him. It was apparently some time before the horses realised they were supposed to take the weight of the heavy vehicle on their quarter breechings and, for several memorable moments, the Speaker's coach looked like making an unscheduled and violent entrance into St. James's Palace!

For most of the 1960s the horizon remained as black as one of Bakewell's horses and when Roy Bird was asked to become secretary of the Shire Horse Society in 1963 both he and almost everyone else thought that his main duties would be those of an undertaker. But somehow, largely no doubt due to the energy of Bird himself and of enthusiastic presidents like John Young and David Kay, the tide slowly but surely began to turn. For instance, demand from America had been virtually non-existent since the Slump but in 1966 a Mr. Arlin Wareing from Blackfoot, Idaho, came over 'in search of a couple of Shires' – and took one back. Jim's Chieftain was his name and his immediate success in Idaho was the first seed of a real American revival. Success breeds success and in 1973 the Horserace Betting Levy Board (set up to help not only racing but all breeds of horses) agreed to subsidise a Shire stallion premium scheme. £3000 was allotted for 1973 and raised next year to £10,000.

Following Mr. Wareing's example over forty American breeders came to the Peterborough show in 1970 and they were also taken on visits to three stables owned by 'old faithful' breweries, including Whitbreads.

Members of Whitbreads together with four other breweries, Young and Co., Watney Mann, Courage and Thwaites, provided the Presidents of the Shire Horse Society, appropriately enough, in the early years of revival from 1963 to 1972. The last was Colonel Bill Whitbread's second year and his cousin Simon had held office in

1961. But far more important than such titles, as they would both agree, had been their breweries' unfailing devotion to the Shire horse even in his darkest days.

So what of the future? The Shire has survived but survival alone is not nearly enough for those who love and admire him. A counter offensive is what they want – an advance to win back some of the ground stolen by tractors, cars and lorries.

Probably, I'm afraid, despite unceasing support from Whitbreads and other breweries, that advance will come, if it comes at all, on the land rather than in the towns. As David Kay of Messrs. Thwaites has demonstrated and as Whitbreads will agree, the Shire is an efficient and economical means of short-haul town delivery – and could almost certainly be made both cheaper and at least as efficient as the lorry. But even if unions and other outside factors permitted that attempt to be made it would only be on a small scale. In the foreseeable future no significant increase in horsedrawn transport is likely to be allowed in the major urban centres of Great Britain.

But on the land no such restrictions apply and, as the cost of tractors and fuel goes up year by year, there are sensible hard-headed men who not only preach but practise the doctrine that the horse's day may come again. Did you, for instance, see on Thames T.V. Frank Cvitanovich's marvellous documentary called 'Violet, Bonny, Beauty, Daisy, Grace – and Geoffrey Morton'? The last name on that list is a truly remarkable man who, some twenty years ago, bought a Shire mare called Violet and started farming a few acres on his own account in Yorkshire. Since then, thanks to Violet and his own determination, he has only ever bought five horses – and has sold three times that many. He has never bought or used a tractor and, as he says, his 'tractors' are breeding their own replacements all the time. 'My mares keep working right up to foaling', Geoffrey Morton says, 'it's better for them – and then in two or three years a foal is ready to work himself.'

Copying techniques perfected in America and Canada Geoffrey can now plough four acres in a day – "or more if we really set about it". He uses a five- or even a six-horse team ploughing two fourteen-inch furrows and in his opinion a tractor would need headlights and excessive hours of work to do much better. If you could learn to manage these big teams, horses, according to Morton's theory, would be an economic proposition even on big farms. "There is no doubt in my mind" he says "that the balance is tipping more and more in favour of the horse."

Well, no doubt your tough, scientific, hard-headed mechanical farmers will scoff at such philosophy and in terms of pounds and pence they may be right. But Geoffrey Morton is not by any means the only one who thinks – and farms – this way. He sounds to me a happy man who has a lovely life and maybe more of us should follow his example.

I N August 1936 something went wrong with Whitbread beer. Of the two directors not away on holiday only one, Bill Whitbread, was in London. The other, Sydney (later Sir Sydney) Nevile, had left for a weekend's sailing in the Channel and it was only with the help of the coastguards that contact could be made with him. When Nevile hurried back to Chiswell Street the two men immediately decided to ask the advice of a distinguished chemist and, to their surprise and horror, the expert in question, a certain Professor Moritz, pronounced that the horses – or rather their fodder – were to blame.

The main stables in those days were actually part of the Brewery at Chiswell Street and in Professor Moritz's opinion the hay kept there had in some way contaminated the beer. Bill Whitbread, himself a keen horseman (later both Chairman of Whitbreads and President of the Shire Horse Society, he rode fifteen winners under National Hunt rules and twice completed the course in the Grand National), has never fully accepted the professor's theory. By 1936 the number of horses at Chiswell Street had been very much reduced from the record figure of 412 employed there at the outbreak of the First World War. So if horses or their hay were, in some mysterious way, going to affect the beer it seemed strange that they had not done so before. At all events, and whatever the truth of the matter, this is, so far as I can discover, the only time the Shires have ever been accused of doing Whitbreads harm as opposed to good! But it was high summer, the height of the beer drinking season, and something had to be done. So Professor Moritz's advice was reluctantly accepted and the Shires were exiled to Garrett Street.

At the start of 1978 there were fifteen geldings on the strength, ranging in age from the seventeen-year-old Rhyme II down to the three latest arrivals who had still not been named when I met them. One of these three, a young grey giant still only five years old, stands no less than eighteen hands two inches. He is in fact too big to lie down in one of the normal stalls and has to sleep in his own downstairs loosebox.

It has always been Whitbread policy to give the Company's Shires a happy, comfortable retirement when they get too old for full-time work in London, and there are now seven 'pensioners' in various good homes around the country. Two of these, Hengist and the first Gilbert (whose original workmate, Sullivan, is still at Garrett Street), are among the chief attractions at the Dodington Carriage Museum near Bath.

They are not actually asked nowadays to pull any of the strange and wonderful vehicles which are exhibited there – among them, would you believe it, an 'Equirotal Phaeton' specially designed for the Duke of Wellington in 1838! (It has four identical wheels and can be divided in the middle to make two separate parts.) But with this marvel, as with most of the other carriages at Dodington, there would be nothing like room for a Shire between the shafts. Though no longer working, Gilbert and Hengist have plenty of company – not only the many human visitors (with whom they are great favourites) but also cattle, goats, pigs, ducks, peacocks and fowl of many other kinds. On a fine day they share the model farmyard at Dodington with all these but, by the look of it, their best friend, or Hengist's anyway, is a furry donkey by the name of Parsley.

The stables, now in Garrett Street, will be moved to the North Yard of the Chiswell Street site when the redevelopment of the seven-acre site is completed in the early 1980s. These, and indeed the whole working life of the Whitbread Shires, are now controlled by Charlie Ruocco who has been with the Company for twenty-eight years. For the last eight of those he has been foreman at Garrett Street with a staff of fifteen under him: six drivers, six stablemen, two blacksmiths and one nightwatchman. Charlie, whose father came to this country from Italy, has worked with horses all his life, starting as a van-boy with the railways nearly fifty years ago. 'We only had *ordinary* horses at the station then,' he says, 'but there were plenty of them. Us boys weren't allowed to drive, of course, but they worked us pretty hard and it was a good way to learn.'

The busy, happy stable over which Charlie now presides is, like the old one at Chiswell Street, built on two storeys. There are two large looseboxes at ground level but the main stables – one on the first floor reached up a tan-strewn ramp – are long, airy rows of open-ended stalls twelve feet long by nine feet wide. To someone accustomed to the closed-in loosebox life of racehorses or hunters it seems strange at first to find that the Shires are tied up both day and night. A rope from their headcollar runs through a hole in the manger and is then knotted at the required length through a retaining block of wood. At night of course the horses need a longer rope allowing them to lie down. But they still remain tied up – or are supposed to – although there are some notable exceptions.

Vim II, for instance, sixteen years old and the only bay in the present team, is widely known as the Garrett Street 'Houdini'. He earned the title by bringing to a fine art his own method of wriggling out of a headcollar or halter. 'You don't often actually *see* him doing it,' Charlie Ruocco says, 'but suddenly there he is walking about as cool as you please – quite loose and delighted with himself,' Nor is Vim the stable's only escapist. Not long ago Hercules, a ten-year-old grey, was found wandering unconcernedly through a busy street market which is held two days a week nearby. According to the stallholder who reported his presence, 'He's doing no harm, mind you. In fact we like having him. I'm just afraid he might get indigestion from all the bits and pieces he's being given . . .'

For the Whitbread Shire in London a normal working day begins about 5.30 a.m. when Charlie Ruocco and the stablemen on duty arrive at Garrett Street. Unlike a conventional loosebox the open-backed stalls have no water bucket so the horses have to be led

out at various times to drink at a trough at the end of each stable. There are incidentally strict rules – still printed on the wall of Charlie's office – against the use, when out at work, of public watering troughs. 'Any infringement of this caution will be followed by instant dismissal' the notice says and even if that fifty-year-old injunction might not be quite so strictly enforced now it shows how seriously the risk of infection was taken in the days when London's streets were swarming with horses of every shape, colour, size and background. The actual times for watering in the stable are, for obvious reasons, fixed so that no horse is asked to go out to work too soon after having a drink.

'The usual hours of work of town horses is not less than ten – and this in all weathers.' Thomas Dykes, who wrote those words in the late nineteenth century, was a Scotsman but a close observer of the heavy horse in London. He knew what he was talking about and there is no reason to doubt his facts or figures. There is even less reason to doubt that he would be amazed – and probably rather shocked – to see the nice, easy, comfortable life which, compared to some of their ancestors, the Whitbread Shires now lead. Of course they still go out 'in all weathers' and of course some of their public and ceremonial appearances involve long hours of travel as well as a good deal of work in strange and sometimes worrying surroundings. But although their daily task of delivering beer to local City pubs demands the same willingness and common sense which a good dray-horse has always needed, it is not, to tell the truth, what Mr. Dykes and his contemporaries would have called 'hard work'.

Although Dykes did not tell us much about the way horses were fed in his time I suspect he would also have admired and envied the modern menu at Garrett Street. By the time the drivers (or draymen) arrive at 7.30 a.m. the Shires have already been mucked out and groomed. They have also had breakfast – the first of three meals which (not counting the nosebag they get while out at work) add up to a total weight of thirty-two pounds a day. With that much corn, chaff, nuts, hay and a cooked mash twice a week, it is no wonder that the Shires' coats gleam with well-upholstered health. There is in fact a certain amount of disagreement at Garrett Street – as there is in stables almost everywhere – about what their ideal diet ought to be. While the stablemen understandably care most about the horses' appearance the draymen, however delighted they may be to have them looking big and well, are also closely and personally concerned with their behaviour! No one man, however strong and skilful, can stop two horses weighing the best part of a ton apiece if they really mean to go. And Shires, though models of calm and good behaviour most of the time, can on occasion 'feel their oats' just as much as any other horse. Charlie Ruocco for instance has a vivid memory of driving a pair of horses across Tower Bridge when, because of some Royal birthday, the guns in the Tower began to fire a salute. 'I never found out whose birthday it was,' says Charlie – 'or how old he may have been. Because by the time they fired the third shot we were off, full tilt, across the bridge. There were traffic lights at the far end and they only turned green in the nick of time. I couldn't have gone a yard slower and it took me half a mile to pull up!'

But happily that sort of nightmare is exceptional. One critic complained in the nineteenth century that the Frisian blood on which Robert Bakewell had partly based his breeding operation was apt to produce 'nasty tempered, unpredictable brutes'. But if

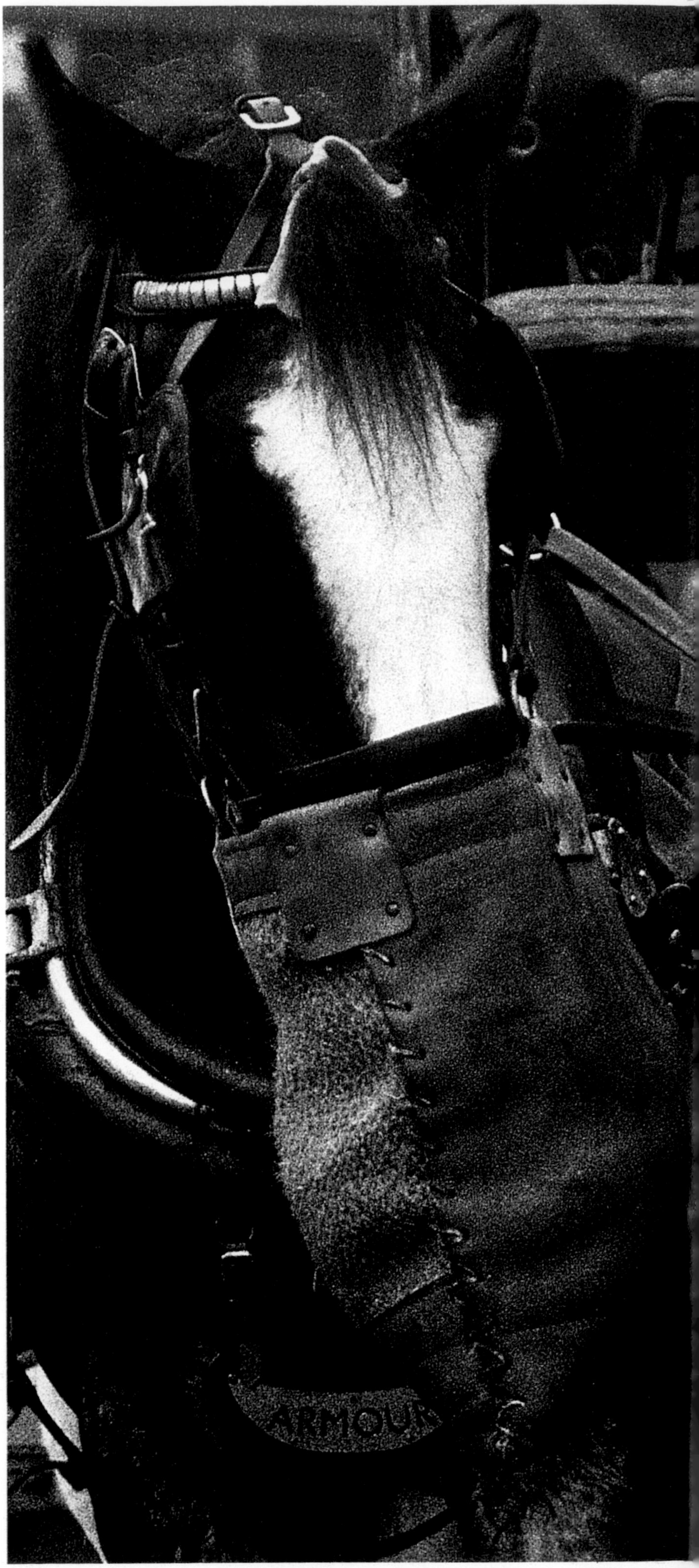

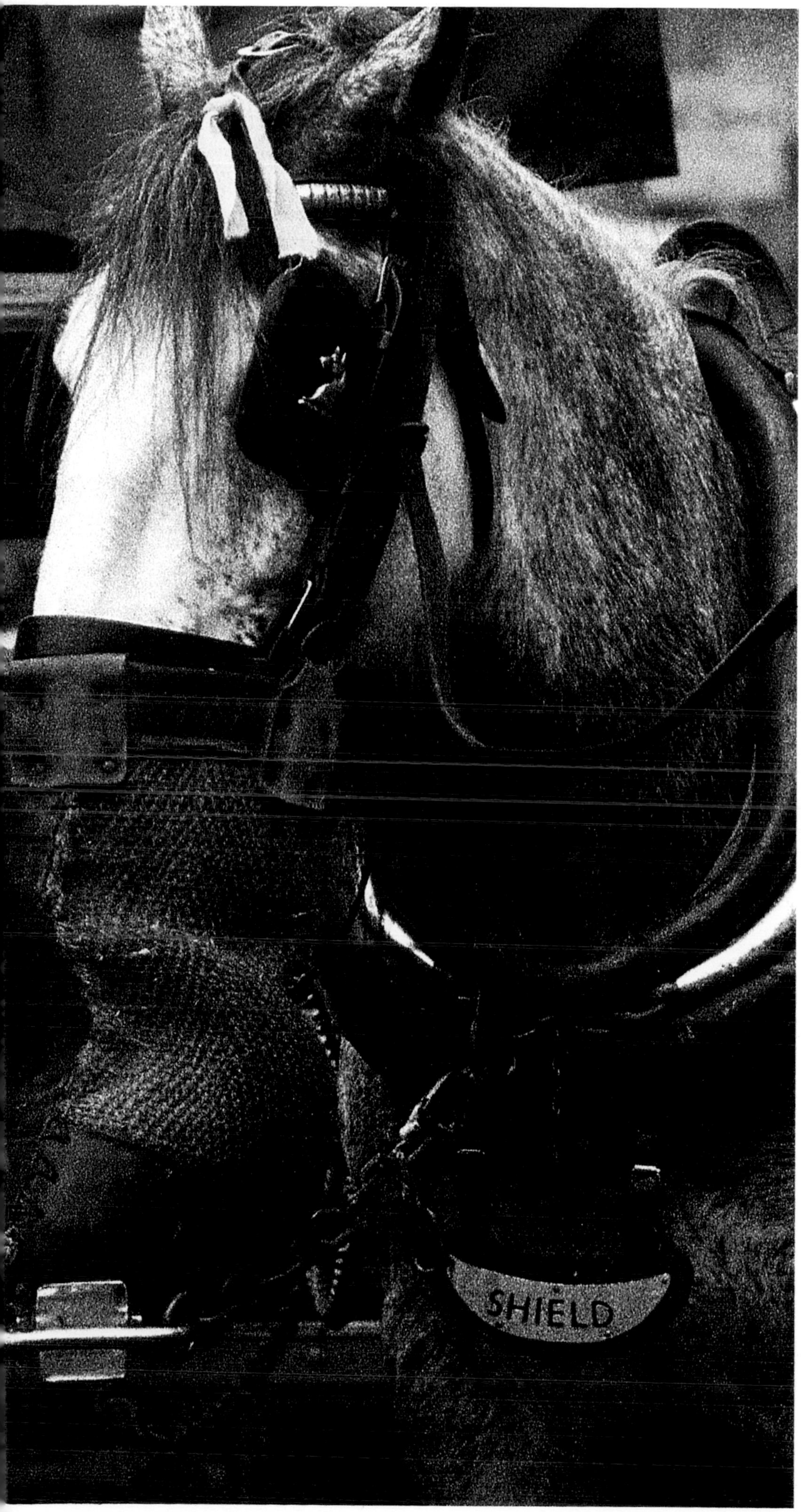

that was ever fair comment it only makes the marvellously imperturbable temperament of the modern Shire a bigger and better advertisement for the skill of those dedicated men who built on the foundations Bakewell laid.

It has for many years been a rule at the Brewery that Whitbread Shires never actually compete at the many shows and functions they attend. 'They are working horses,' Colonel Whitbread says, 'and as long as they do their job properly that is quite enough for us.'

Although other breweries have been heard to criticise this policy you don't have to spend long in the Garrett Street stables to know that the draymen there are at least as proud of their horses as a thousand first-prize rosettes could make them – and maybe even prouder.

'You ought to see how some of those tarted-up show ring marvels carry on,' I was told, 'their men can't leave them alone for ten seconds; we just put ours where we want them and they would stay there all night.' You see this massive patience demonstrated daily in the City during the Shires' normal delivery rounds and although of course individuals differ life in the Garrett Street stable would be impossible if the horses who live and work there were not calm, sensible characters willing to put their great strength gently and cheerfully at mankind's disposal.

Of course they have to be trained, but by the time a Whitbread Shire arrives in London, usually aged four or five, he has already undergone a good deal of careful schooling.

Many of the horses in recent years have either been bred or found and bought for Whitbreads by the famous Derbyshire dealer and breeder Tom Yates. First of all when they are still only two years old – nothing like fully grown and developed – he has them carefully 'mouthed' and introduced to harness. The first thing young horses are actually asked to pull is probably a fairly undemanding chain harrow but then, as three-year-olds, they graduate to rolls, small carts and finally to wagons. By the time they get to Garrett Street in fact they are fairly experienced farm horses – accustomed to a varied five- or six-hour working day.

But the City of London, needless to say, is an entirely different matter. To a young horse fresh from the country the streets seem full of strange, unidentifiable horrors. He must get used to a thousand unfamiliar sights and sounds and smells – to say nothing of the weight and noise of a heavy dray behind him.

Fortunately the dray-horse's job is essentially a partnership and Charlie Ruocco's first move with any new youngster arriving from the country is to choose an older, more experienced 'schoolmaster' companion with whom he can get to know the ropes. On my first visit to the stables Vim had been detailed to instruct a four-year-old grey making only his second venture on the streets. It remains to be seen how much 'Houdini' communicated of his notorious escapist tendencies but in every other respect he was a kindly and tolerant teacher. John Lawless, who was driving the pair, has been with Whitbreads for fourteen years and has been the Lord Mayor's coachman for eight years.

Not many yards out into Garrett Street the young horse, placed, as always, on the near side away from the traffic, suddenly stopped dead, staring down at a manhole cover as though he expected it to bite him or explode. Vim stopped too – because he had to – and very, very quietly John Lawless laid his whip along

the quarters of the grey. It was not in any sense a blow or a punishment. 'What you've got to do,' Charlie Ruocco explains, 'is take his mind off whatever frightened him. Get him thinking about something else and then you mostly find the old horse will carry him along.' Well, on this occasion anyway, Vim and the psychology worked together like a charm. In a moment the two had moved off calmly down the street and only three weeks later I saw the same recruit, paired now with another grey, starting out on his first actual delivery round.

Sometimes, apparently, the education period takes a good deal longer and some horses like some people remain slow learners all their lives. A grey nine-year-old called Pikeman, for instance, is, according to his regular driver Syd Pledger, 'a bit of a goof'. 'He means well but you just can't always trust him not to do something a bit stupid.' By all accounts you cannot *altogether* trust Pikeman's friend and partner Musketeer either. He has once or twice been known to use his hind legs for offensive purposes! But these two were 'wheelers' (the pair closest to the coach in a six-horse team) in the Lord Mayor's show last year. That is not a job for delinquents and even when one of the Whitbread draymen describes some slight shortcoming in his horses there is always affection and pride behind the words.

By the time the horses and men have had their breakfast on a normal weekday morning Charlie Ruocco will have drawn up his list of duties for that day. Two pairs will normally be down to make deliveries, two old horses might be going out instructing youngsters and the rest – barring of course the occasional invalid – are driven round the streets for an hour or so simply for exercise.

Your first impression on entering the Garrett Street yard is its size – or rather lack of it. Down one side, under cover, there stands a row of drays, each twenty-five feet long. There are in fact eight drays, five wagons, one period dray and four other assorted vehicles including, when I was last there, two specially constructed and reinforced 'flat tops' which were to be used as obstacles in the cross-country phase of the Badminton three-day event which is sponsored by Whitbreads. But the normal working drays are, as I say, twenty-five feet long with a pole projecting in front. When you think of their size and that of the animals who are going to pull them it looks a physical impossibility to manoeuvre such a combination in so confined a space.

'Impossible'? After twenty-eight years and a lifetime with horses Charlie Ruocco is entitled to smile. 'Just you watch,' he said, and pointed across to a doorway beside the main gate into Garrett Street. There, padding quietly down the ramp which leads to their first-floor living quarters, Gilbert (the third and latest holder of that name) and Sullivan were coming to start their working day. The morning I first met them Ray Charlesworth was leading Gilbert, with Sullivan following calmly, quite loose behind them. Ray, who served with the Queen's Troop before he joined Whitbreads eleven years ago, would already have checked the dray he was about to use and put on board a bait sack containing the two horses' nosebags and any food he might need for himself. Then, upstairs again, he would lift down the heavy padded collars which hang upside down on pegs beside each horse's stall. They are hoisted gently over the head, still upside down, and then turned round to slip down into place in front of the shoulders. These collars, carefully fitted for each horse, are perhaps the most

important part of all his equipment because it is through them that he takes the main strain of the load. The next step in the morning routine is to put on the rest of the two Shires' working harness with heavy leather-coated chains attached to the hame hook on the collar and breechings round their quarters with which, if necessary, a horse can lean back into the load to stop or slow it down a hill. Lastly Ray puts on the two blinkered bridles with their 'Liverpool' driving bits. Then he oils the horses' hooves, wipes over their eyes and nostrils, and Gilbert and Sullivan are ready for work.

Walking across to his flat-topped four-wheeled dray at the end of the yard, Ray turned Gilbert towards us and without any further gesture or command the big grey backed quietly into position beside the pole. While his chains and reins were being connected Sullivan patiently waited his turn until, spotting an unfamiliar object, he wandered over to me, either curious or hopeful of a present.

When you are accustomed to ordinary horses, a Shire's head seems a very large thing indeed to have thrust, however gently, into your lap. But Sullivan's whole approach was a model of diplomatic courtesy – and he even accepted my regrettable failure to produce a worthwhile titbit without any sign of disappointment. Then, hearing Ray's call, he turned away, walked over to his place and in less than five minutes the whole, to a layman, infinitely complicated business of 'shooting on' or 'putting in' was complete. I cannot attempt to describe to you how the double reins and all the various traces, chains and breechings are connected. But it looks easy in an expert's hands – and the Whitbread draymen make it look like child's play.

And child's play was what Gilbert and Sullivan then proceeded to make of the manoeuvre which I had thought 'impossible'. The moment Ray had climbed aboard and fastened his dicky strap (which you or I might call a safety belt) they turned the dray in its own length, side-stepping in perfect unison, and spun it, with inches to spare on either side, out through the archway into Garrett Street. First stop was the Brewery, where, with only a little more room to spare they backed into the loading bay with the precision of long practice. Then, having taken on a 'trouncer' (as the drayman's mate is called) and a full load of metal kegs, they were off, dancing along so full of themselves on a Monday morning that I almost had to run to keep up.

Ray's first objective was the White Lion in Central Street and, drawing up outside it, he pulled the nosebags from the bait sack and fitted them to Gilbert's and Sullivan's bridles. 'They are not really hungry,' he explained, 'but it gives them something to do – a bit like chewing gum.' Hungry or not, the horses know their job and for the next hour or so they stood, relaxed and perfectly content, taking no notice of the passing traffic and moving nothing but their jaws.

For Ray and his trouncer by contrast the next forty-five minutes were both full and busy. While Ray was fitting the nosebags the trouncer had disappeared like a pantomime demon in reverse, through a trap door in the street. From there he handed up a stream of empty kegs and, with them parked safely on the pavement, he and Ray began unloading. One drops the heavy full kegs onto the 'bumper' (not, in this sense of the word, an amateur jockey but a heavy stuffed hemp sack which is used to protect the

kegs from the street and vice versa) and the other catches
them more or less first bounce.

Then, after loading up the empties, the full kegs had to be
lowered down a chute into the cellar – either 'laced' by a complex
arrangement of rope, or hooked on through a hole in their metal
necks. Either way the man at the top takes the strain so that the kegs
slide down (onto the bumper again) without denting either
themselves or the trouncer.

This was the only delivery Ray had to make that particular day
and after a grateful half pint from the landlord he headed Gilbert
and Sullivan back towards Garrett Street. Watching the passers-
by you could tell that for most of them the dray was a familiar and
reassuring sight – to be greeted often with a smile or a cheerful
wave. Most of the traffic, as Charlie Ruocco had told me, was
equally friendly and helpful. Only one mini-cab driver (who by the
look of his double chin should have been walking) made an
unfriendly contribution – several impatient blasts on his horn and
a couple of shouted epithets to which Gilbert and Sullivan
reacted with dignified disdain.

'They don't really need me,' said Ray with affection, 'they
would go home all by themselves.' He is probably just about right
because in Charlie Ruocco's office there is a newspaper cutting
which tells the story of a six-year-old Whitbread Shire mare called
Gracie. She and her partner Quota were delivering beer in
Shoreditch when their driver Charles Gardner suffered a stroke
just after mounting the dray. With him, semi-conscious and held in
place by his dicky strap but quite unable to help her, Gracie
calmly walked back more than a mile to Garrett Street – crossing
two sets of traffic lights on the way and observing them all
correctly. Outside the stable she whinnied and scraped her feet
until help came and, while I don't quite see why Quota did not
deserve an almost equal share of credit, no one can grudge Gracie
her place on the P.D.S.A.'s Role of Honour.

Deliveries of beer are of course only half the Shires' life – a
leisurely, happy part but dull and unglamorous beside the other.
I have written already of their ceremonial appearances with the
Speaker's and the Lord Mayor's coaches. But quite apart from
those great days, for nine months of the year from February to
October they have an engagement almost every weekend at shows,
processions, festivals and fairs, parades, race meetings, carnivals
and fêtes. On the right you can see the Shires' typical 'diary'.

For two or more Shires and at least two draymen every one of
those dates means a journey, sometimes a long one, new
surroundings, new faces and another chance for the horses to show
their strength, good manners and massive elegance. From
Louvain in Belgium to the showgrounds at Peterborough and Derby
they help to prove that, after the first hundred years of the Society
which was founded to protect and encourage him, the Shire horse
is alive and well in Britain.

Only fifty years ago no one with any sense would have bet
much money on that statement ever being made. But now it can I
think at least be said with confidence that as long as Whitbread
beer is brewed there will be Whitbread Shires.

HORSE DIARY

MARCH

22	Shire Horse Society Centenary Parade, Peterborough
27	The London Harness Horse Parade Society, The Inner Circle, Regent's Park

APRIL

13–16	Badminton (2 pairs)
22	Whitbread Gold Cup, Sandown

MAY

10–30	Belgium Beer Festival Procession in Louvain
21	Rolls Royce Show, Lingfield
29	Centenary Show, Derby

JUNE

3	Ware Carnival Procession
10	Fremlins Sports Day, Kent County Show Ground
19–23	Weymouth
24	Sydenham Gala Day Procession
25	Elstree & Boreham Wood Round Table Donkey Derby
26– 7 July	Torquay and Plymouth

JULY

1	Carnival Parade, Pond Street, Hampstead
2	Lower Marsh, Waterloo
13–15	Kent County Show, County Show Ground
15	Tooting & Balham Carnival
19–20	Shire Horse Centenary, East of England Show (six-horse team)
24–26	Whitbread & Brewery Allied Traders Fair, County Show Ground

AUGUST

6	The All England Jumping Course Parade, Hickstead
9	Basingstoke Rugby Club
13	Whitbread Young Riders Competition, Sevenoaks
19	Folkestone Carnival
28	White Horse Heavy Horse Show, Faringdon, Oxon

SEPTEMBER

3	Burghley Horse Trials
9	Hoddesdon Carnival
10–11	Cheltenham Race Course
16	Cranham Carnival and Fete

OCTOBER

2–7	Horse of The Year Show
14	Faversham Torch Light Carnival
20	Swindon
21	Windsor Parade
30– 1 Nov.	Marlow

NOVEMBER

11	Lord Mayor's Show